The Glorious Kingdom

Cycle B Sermons Based on Second Lessons
for Advent, Christmas, and Epiphany

William Thomas

CSS Publishing Company
Lima, Ohio

THE GLORIOUS KINGDOM

FIRST EDITION
Copyright © 2023
by CSS Publishing Co., Inc.

Published by CSS Publishing Company, Inc., Lima, Ohio 45807. All rights reserved. No part of this publication may be reproduced in any manner whatsoever without the prior permission of the publisher, except in the case of brief quotations embodied in critical articles and reviews. Inquiries should be addressed to: CSS Publishing Company, Inc., Permissions Department, 5450 N. Dixie Highway, Lima, Ohio 45807.

Library of Congress Cataloging-in-Publication Data:

Names: Thomas, William (Evangelist), author.
Title: The glorious kingdom : Cycle B sermons based on the second lessons for Advent, Christmas, and epiphany / William Thomas.
Description: First edition. | Lima, Ohio : CSS Publishing Company, [2023] | Includes bibliographical references.
Identifiers: LCCN 2023015231 (print) | LCCN 2023015232 (ebook) | ISBN 9780788030802 | ISBN 9780788030819 (ebook)
Subjects: LCSH: Advent sermons. | Christmas sermons. | Epiphany season--Sermons.
Classification: LCC BV4254.5 .T48 2023 (print) | LCC BV4254.5 (ebook) | DDC 252/.612--dc23/eng/20230731
LC record available at https://lccn.loc.gov/2023015231
LC ebook record available at https://lccn.loc.gov/2023015232

For more information about CSS Publishing Company resources, visit our website at www.csspub.com, email us at csr@csspub.com, or call (800) 241-4056.

e-book:
ISBN-13: 978-0-7880-3081-9
ISBN-10: 0-7880-3081-7

ISBN-13: 978-0-7880-3080-2
ISBN-10: 0-7880-3080-9

PRINTED IN USA

Contents

Introduction 7

First Sunday of Advent: 1 Corinthians 1:3-9
Invited Into His Kingdom 9

Second Sunday of Advent: 2 Peter 3:8-15a
He Is Coming 13

Third Sunday of Advent: 1 Thessalonians 5:16-24
Sanctified And Ready 17

Fourth Sunday of Advent: Romans 16:25-27
Gospel Realized 20

Nativity of the Lord Proper 1: Titus 2:11-14
Grace And Glory 23

Nativity of the Lord Proper II: Titus 3:4-7
Rebirth And Renewal 26

Nativity of the Lord-Proper III: Hebrews 1:1-4, (5-12)
Superior To All 30

First Sunday After Christmas Day: Galatians 4:4-7
We Are Family 34

Baptism of the Lord: Acts 19:1-7
Entering The Kingdom 37

Second Sunday after the Epiphany: 1 Corinthians 6:12-20
Prepare Our Bodies For The Kingdom 40

Third Sunday after the Epiphany: 1 Corinthians 7:29-31
The Time Is Short 43

Fourth Sunday after the Epiphany: 1 Corinthians 8:1-13
Sacrifice For The Kingdom's Sake 47

Presentation of the Lord: Hebrews 2:14-18
He Became One Of Us 50

Fifth Sunday after the Epiphany: 1 Corinthians 9:16-23
For The Sake Of The Gospel 53

Transfiguration Sunday: 2 Corinthians 4:3-6
The Glory Of Christ 56

I want to thank David Runk and CSS Publishing for allowing me the chance to write and share what matters most to me.

A big "Thank You" also goes out to all the churches to whom I have preached. The congregations at Stony Point, Northridge, FCC Washington, and Higbee Baptist have encouraged me more than they will ever know.

I also want to thank Cindy Bingamon for her diligence and thoughtful reading of the proofs to make sure the final copy was as clean as it could be.

Most of all, I want to thank Jesus Christ, my Lord and Savior. He is truly the King of Kings.

Introduction

Max Lucado wrote, "God goes to those who have time to hear him — and so on this cloudless night he went to simple shepherds."[1] That message resonates at this Christmas season. As he sent angels to shepherds a long time ago, God is reaching out today to those who listen. The message is just as clear today as it was then. "Today in the town of David a Savior has been born to you; he is the Messiah, the Lord. This will be a sign to you: You will find a baby wrapped in cloths and lying in a manger" (Luke 2:11-12).

A Savior has been born. Messiah has come. Of this, Isaiah foretold, "For to us a child is born, to us a son is given, and the government will be on his shoulders. And he will be called Wonderful Counselor, Mighty God, Everlasting Father, Prince of Peace. Of the greatness of his government and peace there will be no end. He will reign on David's throne and over his kingdom, establishing and upholding it with justice and righteousness from that time on and forever. The zeal of the Lord Almighty will accomplish this" (Isaiah 9:6-7).

The birth of Jesus is significant in many ways. It demonstrates God's love for fallen humanity. It reveals the plan of salvation and the remedy for sin. Jesus' birth fulfills generations of prophecy. His birth also is vital in establishing his kingdom.

I'm convinced that, from the beginning, God has wanted a personal, intimate relationship with human beings he created in his own image. Patrick Schreiner posits that God intended that kind of kingdom with Adam and Eve. He wrote, "The kingdom plan was corrupted when a rival kingdom slithered into the ear of Eve and Adam. The vice-regents, who were to carry out God's blueprint for all of creation, chose to follow the serpent and personally offend the king of the universe. Now chaos and sin frustrate the desire to rule the earth and subdue it. False kingdoms are instantly part of the picture. Every generation afterward will face the same choice: which kind of kingdom will they construct?"[2]

That's the question for us this Christmas season? We are invited to be a part of the glorious kingdom of Jesus Christ. Is there anything

---

1 Max Lucado, *God Came Near* (Nashville, TN: Thomas Nelson Publishers, 2010), 4.
2 Patrick Schreiner, *The Kingdom of God and the Glory of the Cross* (Wheaton, IL: Crossway Books, 2018), 21.

more important than that? The Bible passages in this series point to Jesus and his glorious kingdom. It is my prayer that each one who encounters them will encounter the one of whom it is said, "his kingdom will never end" (Luke 1:33).

First Sunday of Advent
1 Corinthians 1:3-9

Invited Into His Kingdom

Grace to you and peace from God our Father and the Lord Jesus Christ.

I give thanks to my God always for you because of the grace of God that has been given you in Christ Jesus, for in every way you have been enriched in him, in speech and knowledge of every kind — just as the testimony of Christ has been strengthened among you — so that you are not lacking in any spiritual gift as you wait for the revealing of our Lord Jesus Christ. He will also strengthen you to the end, so that you may be blameless on the day of our Lord Jesus Christ. God is faithful; by him you were called into the fellowship of his Son, Jesus Christ our Lord.

Receiving an invitation is exciting. In his book, *Love Does: Discover a Secretly Incredible Life in an Ordinary World,* Bob Goff wrote about sneaking on to the set of the movie *National Treasure 2*. Goff and his friend Brandon were in Washington DC on business. Around midnight near Capitol Hill, they saw a bunch of cars awkwardly parked around the Library of Congress. Barricades were set up, so they decided to investigate. They discovered that it was a set for the filming of *National Treasure 2*. They looked at each other as a plan formed. They ran back to their hotel and changed from their suits to blue jeans and t-shirts to look the part of the film crew. They then went back, dodged a couple of security guards, ran across a couple of lawns and through some bushes. They finally got to the side entrance where the crew went in and walked right in as if they belonged there and nobody said a thing. They followed the signs and arrows that said, "Set" on them. They arrived at a metal detector with a guard standing by it. Surprisingly, he let them in without badges. They turned a few corners until they found themselves on the set, in the middle of the Library of Congress. As they watched for a moment or two, they began to plan their escape. Suddenly Nicholas Cage and Diane Kruger rounded the corner and without even thinking, they fell into their entourage as if they belonged and walked right out without a question being asked and had another thrilling adventure.

Goff then wrote, "There are a lot of things I don't get invited to. I've never been invited to the Oscars or Paul McCartney's birthday or to a space shuttle launch. I'm waiting for my invitation to the *National Treasure 3*. If I got an invitation to any of those, I'd definitely go. There's nothing like feeling included."[3]

"There's nothing like feeling included." That statement resounds from the text today. As we start this Advent season, we are not like Charlie Brown, in the 1965 Peanuts *A Charlie Brown Christma*" whose mailbox contained no Christmas cards. We have received a card, an invitation if you will. We are called to be a part of the kingdom of God. "God is faithful; by him you were called into the fellowship of his Son, Jesus Christ our Lord" (1 Corinthians 1:9). The word translated "called" can also be understood "invited." You and I have an invitation to the greatest thing imaginable.

Preparations Are Made
In verses four through six, Paul makes it clear that the Corinthian believers are prepared. He's already stated his thankfulness for them. They have been recipients of God's grace through Jesus Christ. He begins noting how they are prepared by acknowledging that, through Jesus, they have been enriched in every way, in both speech and knowledge. The word for "enriched" here indicates a sense of having been made full or complete. Additionally, the testimony of Jesus is confirmed or strengthened among them.

These believers, through the grace of God expressed in Jesus are ready for the coming of his kingdom. Like the Corinthian believers, we are also prepared for the coming of God's kingdom. Through the grace of God given to us in Jesus we are enriched or made complete in every way. Our lives can reflect the grace of Jesus to the world around us that is desperate to see it. Having received an invitation to be a part of his kingdom and waiting for his coming (celebrating the first and anticipating the second) we have the chance to live in a way that points to the kingdom.

A story is told of a young salesman who was disappointed about losing a big sale. Dejectedly, he talked with his sales manager lamenting, "I guess it just proves you can lead a horse to water, but you can't

3 Bob Goff, *Love Does: Discover a Secretly Incredible Life in an Ordinary World* (Nashville, TN: Thomas Nelson Publishers, 2012), 77-78.

make him drink." The manager replied, "Your job is not to make him drink. Your job is to make him thirsty." That's what kingdom lives do in the world around them. They create a hunger and thirst for righteousness.

To you it may have only been a quick morning exchange of pleasantries, but to a lonely neighbor it was a reminder that someone cares.

To you it might have been just playing catch with the neighbor kid for a while after work, but to the child, it was a day in which an adult chose to interact positively with them.

To you it was only a few dollars, but to the desperate man on the corner it was a hot meal and an affirmation of his humanity.

As we await the celebration of his first coming, remember, we are prepared to live lives that point to his kingdom.

Wait Expectantly Relying On Him

Verse seven indicated that the Corinthian believers lacked nothing with respect to spiritual gifts while they waited for the Lord. Verse eight noted that Jesus would strengthen them so that they could be blameless. Two things emerge from this passage. First, the Corinthian believers were to wait expectantly. They were not to wait, hoping that Jesus will come. They were to wait, knowing that Jesus will come. They were to trust in God's faithfulness. They would wait, but not in a nervous uncertainty. Second, the ability to live blamelessly (lives that point to the kingdom) would come from the Lord himself.

We get the strength to live in a way that points to the kingdom from Jesus. We can't do it by ourselves. Our best intentions and plans will leave us woefully short of what might have been. To be the witness the world needs, we must rely on the power of the Lord at work in us.

A.W. Tozer said, "God is looking for people through whom he can do the impossible. What a pity that we plan only the things we can do by ourselves."[4] The Lord will equip us to do what needs to be done. He gives us the strength to forgive what others deem unforgiveable. He empowers us to stand firm when most would have run away. He strengthens us to endure when others would have quit. He emboldens us to act when others would have ignored.

The ability to live effective lives that point to the kingdom comes from the Lord. We can't do it on our own. We need him.

We are invited to be citizens of the greatest kingdom the world has ever known. We can rejoice in that. He has also prepared us to live

---

4 Tom Jones, *Church Planting from the Ground Up* (Joplin, MO: College Press, 2004), 104.

effective lives that point to that kingdom while we wait for it. As we approach the celebration of his first Advent, ask yourself, "What are people seeing in me?" "To what is my life pointing?" Amen.

Second Sunday of Advent
2 Peter 3:8-15a

He Is Coming

But do not ignore this one fact, beloved, that with the Lord one day is like a thousand years, and a thousand years are like one day. The Lord is not slow about his promise, as some think of slowness, but is patient with you, not wanting any to perish, but all to come to repentance. But the day of the Lord will come like a thief, and then the heavens will pass away with a loud noise, and the elements will be dissolved with fire, and the earth and everything that is done on it will be disclosed.

Since all these things are to be dissolved in this way, what sort of persons ought you to be in leading lives of holiness and godliness, waiting for and hastening the coming of the day of God, because of which the heavens will be set ablaze and dissolved, and the elements will melt with fire? But, in accordance with his promise, we wait for new heavens and a new earth, where righteousness is at home.

Therefore, beloved, while you are waiting for these things, strive to be found by him at peace, without spot or blemish; and regard the patience of our Lord as salvation.

While not necessarily a well-known hymn, the message of the hymn "Hold the Fort" is a powerful one. Philip Bliss wrote the hymn "Hold the Fort" in 1870. Just before General William T. Sherman began his famous march to the sea in 1864, and while his army lay camped near Atlanta, Georgia, on October 5, the army of Confederate General Hood, in a carefully prepared movement, passed the right flank of Sherman's army and began the destruction of the railroad leading north, burning blockhouses, and capturing the small garrisons along the line. Sherman's army was put in rapid motion pursuing Hood, to save the supplies and larger posts, the principal one of which was located at Altoona Pass. That is where General John Corse of Illinois was stationed with about fifteen hundred men.

Rebels surrounded the post and demanded surrender. Corse refused and a sharp fight commenced. The defenders were slowly driven into a small fort on the crest of the hill. The fight looked hopeless. At this moment an officer caught sight of a white signal flag about twenty miles away. The message was clear: "Hold the fort; I am coming. W. T. Sherman."[5]

The message "hold the fort" is one we understand. As we enter the Christmas season, we are reminded of his first coming. The celebration of his first coming, though, must be connected to the fact of his second coming. The glorious kingdom of our Lord Jesus Christ is begun at his first Advent and inaugurated at his second. There are three important truths that we need to recognize as we wait for his coming. First, his coming back will catch some by surprise. Second, as we wait, we are to live holy lives. Finally, pay attention while we wait. We have an opportunity to share the news of Jesus before he returns.

It Will Come As A Surprise
The second advent of Jesus will surprise some who are not paying attention. That day will "come like a thief" (v. 10). This phrase "like a thief" points to the suddenness and unexpectedness of his coming. Despite the evidence of history and the words of the prophets, there are many who live out their lives without any thought for what is to come.

In the fall of 1941, most Americans believed that the war in the Pacific was far from them and not their concern. Donald Stratton wrote, "Clarke Beach, for example, in a September 6 article for the local newspaper, the *Star-Bulletin*, wrote, 'A Japanese attack on Hawaii is regarded as the most unlikely thing in the world, with one chance in a million of being successful.'"[6] A Japanese attack on Hawaii was unthinkable until it happened on December 7, 1941. Just as many were surprised on that December day long ago, many will be surprised at the coming of Jesus.

We Are Called To Be Holy
We must be ready. The fact of his return is not something that should strike fear in our hearts. Paul's words provide a different mindset.

---

5   "Hold the Fort," *Hymn Studies Blog*, August 9, 2016, https://hymnstudiesblog.wordpress.com/2016/08/09/hold-the-fort/

6   Donald Stratton, *All the Gallant Men: An American Sailor's First-Hand Account of Pearl Harbor* (New York, NY: Mariner Books, 2016)

"Do not be anxious about anything, but in everything by prayer and supplication with thanksgiving let your requests be made known to God. And the peace of God, which surpasses all understanding, will guard your hearts and your minds in Christ Jesus" (Philippians 4:6-7). With the peace of God guarding our hearts, we are to live holy lives while we wait.

Waiting can be hard without something to do. We are to live holy lives. In thinking about that, I was drawn to weasels. I know that sounds ridiculous but stay with me. There is quite a bit of research on the ermine, the pristine white animal of the weasel family. While there is considerable discussion about this animal, it does seem that hunters and ermines have an unusual relationship.

Consider the strange story of the ermine told in *Our Daily Bread*. In the forests of northern Europe, the ermine is known for his snow-white fur in winter. It is said he instinctively protects his white coat against anything that would soil it. Fur hunters take advantage of this unusual trait of the ermine. They don't set a trap to catch it. Instead, they find his home, which is usually a cleft in a rock or a hollow in an old tree. The hunter smears the entrance and interior with grime, then sets his dogs loose to find the ermine. The frightened animal flees toward home but doesn't enter because of the filth. Rather than soil his white coat, he is trapped by the dogs and captured while preserving his purity. For the ermine, purity is more precious than life.[7]

That story is puzzling, and it did make me think. How much does purity matter to me? How important is it that I am living a holy life? What would I be willing to lose to maintain purity and holy living?

We Are To Be Watchful

The last thing this passage tells us to do as we wait is pay attention. This is our opportunity to tell others the good news. There are so many people around us who need to hear the good news.

Fanny Crosby, the hymnwriter, paid attention to those around her. In 1869, Fanny J. Crosby wrote the hymn, "Rescue the Perishing" after she met the men who were housed in a New York City mission. She was concerned about their spiritual well-being and pleaded with them if there was someone who had "wandered from his mother's home and teaching," to please come and see her at the end of the service. A young man came up to Crosby and said that he would like to see his

---

7 *Our Daily Bread*, April 21, 1997.

mother in heaven, but according to the way he was living his life, he was convinced it was not possible. After ardent prayer with Crosby and everyone attending the service, he accepted God's grace. That night, Crosby wrote the words to "Rescue the Perishing."[8]

There are people around us that need rescuing, too. Those who are caught in the web of deceit the world spins need help. Those who are weary and broken under the weight of guilt, heartache and defeat need an answer. Even those who don't think they need a thing need Jesus. Will we pay attention? Will we attempt to rescue? This is the day of salvation.

Jesus is coming. Just as he did at the first Advent, he will return. Will we be ready? Will we "hold the fort" until he comes?

Amen.

---

8 Carlton R. Young. *Companion to the United Methodist Hymnal* (Nashville, Abingdon Press, 1993), 568.

Third Sunday of Advent
1 Thessalonians 5:16-24

Sanctified And Ready

Rejoice always, pray without ceasing, give thanks in all circumstances, for this is the will of God in Christ Jesus for you. Do not quench the Spirit. Do not despise prophecies, but test everything; hold fast to what is good; abstain from every form of evil.

May the God of peace himself sanctify you entirely and may your spirit and soul and body be kept sound and blameless at the coming of our Lord Jesus Christ. The one who calls you is faithful, and he will do this.

One of the most important things to remember when buying Christmas gifts is to include getting batteries for the electronic gifts you buy. Nothing is more frustrating than to have a wonderful gift that just sits there because it has no power to make it work. Don't forget the batteries. Don't forget the power. What is true with electronic Christmas gifts is true for Christians as we wait for the second coming of Jesus. The power, the ability to do that comes from our being sanctified or made holy. The word used in verse twenty-three for "sanctify" is from the root word "hagiazó," which means "to make holy." The reason for why we need to be sanctified is also found in verse 24. It is so that our "spirit, soul, and body be kept sound and blameless at his coming." Paul challenges his readers to live a holy life.

The church today reads these same challenges as we are waiting for Jesus' return. Paul is adamant that Jesus will come again (1 Thessalonians 5:23). Death, pain, suffering, and heartache do not get the last word. We wait for a Savior who has conquered death and disarmed his gruesome companions. This period of waiting, though, is not to be idle time. We are called to be sanctified and to trust.

Be Sanctified

What does that holy, sanctified life look like? The preceding verses give us some insight. Rejoice always. Pray without ceasing. Give thanks in all circumstances. Don't quench the Spirit or despise prophecies. Hold on to what is good and stay away from all that is evil. Almost in bullet-point fashion, Paul defines the holy life God wants his people to live. Our lives, as followers of Jesus, are to be examples until the day Jesus returns to take us home. We are to be sanctified and ready when that day comes.

To be holy is to be set apart as different. John MacArthur wrote, "That the issue of sanctification — holiness — weighed so heavily on the heart of the apostle is a fitting reminder to pastors and church members alike that we must not forget what God is doing with us. It is our duty as believers 'to put on the new self, created after the likeness of God in true righteousness and holiness.'"[9]

In the Sermon on the Mount, Jesus talked of being salt and light. Light is a powerful thing. Light is something that can have a dramatic effect on everything it touches. Light makes it possible to see. A lighthouse warns ships of the coastline. An emergency light warns drivers of a problem with the car. Light can bring security and reassurance. When we are in a dark house and hear an unfamiliar noise, we instinctively turn on a light because we want to be able to see and be seen. As we wait for the return of Jesus, we are to be holy, we are to be a light in a world shrouded by darkness. Allow the Spirit of God to work in our hearts.

Imagine a child with her playdough. She pounds, stretches, and shapes that clay into what she wants it to become. The clay cannot refuse to be what the child desires it to be. That's how we are to be with the Spirit of God. Allow him to pound, shape, and stretch us into what he wants us to become.

Things around us seem to be falling apart. There are shootings, violence, senseless killing, hate, anger, division, war, and a host of other horrific acts that saturate our newsfeeds and stain the soul of our nation and world. If there ever was a time when the world needed a Christian influence and example, that time is now.

Trust

Paul also made it clear in this passage that we are to trust that God will do what he has promised to do. He wrote, "The one who calls you is faithful, and he will do this." (v. 24). The word for "faithful" here comes from the Greek word "pistos" which means "worthy of trust." We can trust that God will send Jesus back. He will come. We can trust

---

9 John MacArthur, *Sanctification: God's Passion for His People* (Wheaton, IL: Crossway Books, 2020), 23.

that God will sanctify us. We can trust that God will keep us sound, secure, and blameless. We can trust that God will do what he says he will do.

At a small hotel swimming pool years ago, I saw something that came to mind again as I thought about trust. A little girl was learning to swim. Her older brother and dad were helping her. Mom was sitting in a poolside chair, reading a book. The girl's father held her and had her kick her feet and use her arms. Her brother gave her a demonstration of swimming. She was doing well. The next lesson they wanted to teach her was to jump into the deep end of the pool. She had no trouble being in the shallow end. She could touch the bottom. Now, though, they wanted her to jump in the deep end and do what she'd been taught. To alleviate her fears, her dad jumped in first and swam. Her brother jumped in next and swam. She, however, stood at the edge, petrified to move. Her dad and her brother both called out to her, encouraging her to jump, but she refused. After much cajoling, she told them she would only jump if her dad was treading water nearby. He moved to the deep end, and she jumped. He was able to catch her as she entered the water and pull her up. She swam to the shallow end. Later, she told them she was not afraid to jump because she knew her dad was right there. She knew she'd be safe.

We wait for the coming of our Lord, and while we wait, we live out our faith. We trust that our doing so is not in vain. God, our Father, is right there. He will keep his word and keep us safe until Jesus comes. We can trust God. He will do what he's promised.

Jesus is coming again. At his first Advent, most people were not looking for it and not ready. They were unprepared for the coming of the king. Are we prepared today?

Amen.

Fourth Sunday of Advent
Romans 16:25-27

Gospel Realized

Now to God who is able to strengthen you according to my gospel and the proclamation of Jesus Christ, according to the revelation of the mystery that was kept secret for long ages but is now disclosed and through the prophetic writings is made known to all the gentiles, according to the command of the eternal God, to bring about the obedience of faith — to the only wise God, through Jesus Christ, to whom be the glory forever! Amen.

Busy Tourist website reports that Yellowstone National Park is rated the number one breathtaking paradise for those who love the outdoors. It spans almost 3,500 square miles, and is a trove of steep canyons, incredible mountains, gorgeous waterfalls, and fascinating geysers. It is also populated with teeming wildlife, such as elk, grizzly bears, and buffalo. Additionally, it is home to the rainbow-sheened Grand Prismatic Spring, which is deeper than ten stories and the third largest spring on the planet.[10] Though I have never seen Yellowstone National Park, there is something appealing and breathtaking about magnificent things. Today, we celebrate the magnificent. Jesus' coming is far greater than the wondrous beauty of creation. The last few verses of the book of Romans speaks to the amazing gift God gave us.

Paul concludes this letter to the believers in Rome with a blessing, assuring them of their hope in Christ. This is Paul's longest letter, and much of it is devoted to the hope we have in the gospel. Because of Jesus Christ, we can live by faith daily in the resurrection power of Jesus and experience a fulfilled and hopeful life. We can look back and celebrate his first coming with joy and awe because of the rich life he gives us now. We can also look confidently to his second coming because he continues to give us strength.

---

[10] "50 Most Beautiful Places in The US To Visit in Your Lifetime," Busy Tourist, March 19, 2022, https://www.busytourist.com/most-beautiful-places-in-the-us/

Stand Strong

Paul starts out by proclaiming that God can "strengthen you according to my gospel and the proclamation of Jesus Christ, according to the revelation of the mystery that was kept secret for long ages." Paul has been reminding the believers throughout this letter that everything they need for salvation and for a righteous life has been provided to them in Christ. The law has been fulfilled through Christ, and faith in Christ is the only way to be righteous before God. Next, Paul is telling them the mystery is revealed: that message is for Jews and Gentiles. God's Son is for the world!

Like the Christians in Rome, we can look back to Jesus and see that in him we have all we need. That allowed them and us to stand strong. Jesus Christ is all that we need. We celebrate that at his first coming and anticipate the glory of this return. It's all about Jesus. Different people of different backgrounds, races and status can know the love of God and the wonder of the Savior, Jesus Christ.

The source of this story is unknown, though I found it in several different journals. It's about John Newton, the author of *Amazing Grace*. It is said that John Newton was a rough, dirty sailor with a foul mouth who lived a wretched life. At one point, he was captain of a slave ship. Then someone placed in his hands a copy of Thomas à Kempis' *The Imitation of Christ*. He also had the gift of a good mother who told him about the Savior when he was young. Her prayers and the reading of Kempis' book brought him to Jesus. He went all over England sharing his faith. As he aged, he had to have an assistant stand in the pulpit with him on Sundays. He was nearly blind and spoke in whispers, but nothing could keep him from preaching while he still had breath.

One Sunday, while delivering his message he repeated the sentence: "Jesus Christ is precious." His helper whispered to him: "But you have already said that twice." Newton turned to his helper and said loudly, "Yes, I've said it twice, and I'm going to say it again." The stones in the ancient sanctuary fairly shook as the old preacher said again: "Jesus Christ is precious!"

> Jesus is greater than our wealth.
> Jesus is greater than our position and status.
> Jesus is greater than what the world says divides us.
> Jesus is greater than our possessions.
> Jesus is greater than our education.

Is there anything Jesus is not greater than? Look back and marvel at his humble birth. The King of kings born in an obscure place, sleeping in a feeding trough. It appears to be anything but spectacular, but that's God usual way. "For it is written, 'I will destroy the wisdom of the wise, and the discernment of the discerning I will thwart'" (1 Corinthians 1:9). God acts in ways beyond our understanding. Look back today in awe and wonder of the child of Bethlehem. After looking back, look ahead. He's coming back. We can have that same sense of awe and joy at the anticipation of his return.

Give Him Glory
Paul concludes the letter to the Roman Christians, "to the only wise God, through Jesus Christ, to whom be the glory forever! Amen." This is the conclusion to the doxology. The word "doxa," the word used for "glory" here (and from which we get the English word "doxology) means recognizing the intrinsic or inherent worth of God. Paul is reminding the Roman Christians that the right response to all that God has done for them in Jesus Christ is to praise him. How can we not do the same?

Our Daily Bread shares this story about Abraham Lincoln. Despite a heavy schedule of appointments, President Abraham Lincoln consented to let an elderly woman with no official business in mind visit him in the oval office. As she entered, he rose to greet her and asked how he might be of service. She replied that she had not come to ask a favor. She'd heard that the president liked a certain kind of cookie, so she had baked some for him and brought them to his office. With tears in his eyes, Lincoln responded, "You are the very first person who has ever come into my office asking not, expecting not, but rather bringing me a gift. I thank you from the bottom of my heart."[11]

I wonder if, sometimes, God may feel like President Lincoln did. So many times, we bring to him our needs and wants, and there's nothing wrong with that. I am curious, though, how many times do we simply approach him to praise him? How often do we come in his presence to give him glory?

May we, as we celebrate Jesus' first coming, recognize with awe and humility, the gift God has given the world. May we also look ahead with excitement at his return. As we do both, let us praise him. Amen.

---

11 *Our Daily Bread*, June 4, 1997.

Nativity of the Lord Proper 1
Titus 2:11-14

Grace And Glory

For the grace of God has appeared, bringing salvation to all, training us to renounce impiety and worldly passions and in the present age to live lives that are self-controlled, upright, and godly, while we wait for the blessed hope and the manifestation of the glory of our great God and Savior, Jesus Christ. He it is who gave himself for us that he might redeem us from all iniquity and purify for himself a people of his own who are zealous for good deeds.

Born to save. That's the summation of Jesus' first Advent. Born to save. It is a story that resonates with grace. It is not only the story of Jesus, but also the story of Marissa Ayala. Marissa and her older sister, Anissa appeared on the cover to *Time* magazine in 1991. Their story was the subject of a 1993 made-for-TV movie, "For the Love of My Child: The Anissa Ayala Story."

In 1988, Anissa Ayala was sixteen years-old and diagnosed with a rare form of leukemia. The doctors said that if she did not receive a bone marrow transplant after chemotherapy and radiation treatment she would die. Neither her parents nor her brother was a match, and no other donor could be found. Her parents, both in their forties, conceived another child and hoped that its bone marrow would be compatible with Anissa's. That child was Marissa. At fourteen-months-old Marissa's bone marrow was given to Anissa, who made a full recovery from the leukemia. The family is doing well today, and Anissa and Marissa are exceptionally close. In an article in *The Orange County Register*, Marissa says, "She's like my second mom. We get closer every year."[12]

Born to save. It is a powerful story. In just a few verses, Paul reveals for us the purpose of Jesus' coming. The essence of God's unfolding

---

[12] Greg Hardesty, "The baby born to save her sister says she has no regrets" *The Orange County Register*, July 21, 2008.

plan of salvation is shown in both appearances of Jesus. He writes, "For the grace of God has appeared, bringing salvation to all" (2:11). Jesus' first coming revealed the grace of God. The second advent or coming will emphasize his glory. Paul observes this as he urges Christians to live godly lives "while we wait for the blessed hope and the manifestation of the glory of our great God and Savior, Jesus Christ" (2:13). Born to save is about God's grace and God's glory.

God's Grace

God's grace appeared in the person of Jesus Christ to offer salvation to everyone. This is an important truth. There is no one for whom Jesus Christ did not come. The good news is that no sinner is beyond the grasp of God's grace.

I'll call him Joe. I met Joe in one of the churches I served. He was incredibly intelligent, articulate and when I met him, dedicated to the Lord. It had not always been that way, though. His testimony was powerful. Joe had a career in banking before I met him. His work ethic and talent allowed him to quickly climb the ladder of success. He was a vice-president when he devised an elaborate plan to embezzle money. The plan was brilliant and worked well. However, the more he took, the more he wanted. His greed led to him being caught. He was tried, convicted, and spent ten years in prison. During that time, Joe encountered Jesus through a prison ministry. Though he was guilty of white-collar crime and stealing thousands of dollars, he found forgiveness and acceptance in Jesus. He gave his life to Jesus, receiving the grace he did not deserve. Upon his release, he began to serve Jesus. His testimony stays with me today. "I discovered nothing I ever did put me beyond the reach of God's grace."

What was true for Joe is also true for you. Paul reminds us that his first advent is about the grace of God.

God's Glory

Paul urged Christians to live godly lives while they waited for Jesus' second coming. This coming would highlight the glory of God. It is a fascinating contrast: Christians waiting in a fallen world, saturated by sin and despair. The glory is a reminder of the promise of God. There is a better world coming. William Carey once said, "The future is as bright as the promises of God."

I am a fan of the 1989 movie *Glory*. The movie tells the true story of the 54th Massachusetts Infantry Regiment. Colonel Robert Gould Shaw led the 54th, one of the first all-black units in the Civil War. Their story was amazing. At the beginning, the 54th faced prejudice, hatred, and resentment. They were marginalized by arrogant Union commanders. It was an ugly time. At the end of the movie, though, Colonel Shaw volunteered the 54th to lead the assault on Fort Wagner. It was a brutal assignment. As they marched to the front of the lines on July 18, 1863, they were noticed by all the white regiments, some of whom had earlier ridiculed them. This time, however, there was only honor and respect for the men of the 54th. The glory of being men was realized for the troops of the 54th.

There will come a day when the ugliness, sinfulness, and awfulness of this world will be gone. The second coming of Jesus will usher in the glory of God. Can you imagine how that day will be? As we celebrate the first coming of Jesus and await the second, Paul challenges Christians.

What Now?
In between these two wonderful attributes of God, we are to live to honor and please God. Our relationships with each another, with the communities in which we live, and with the world should reflect the love of God in Jesus Christ, "he it is who gave himself for us that he might redeem us from all iniquity and purify for himself a people of his own who are zealous for good deeds." (2:14).

We have the chance to demonstrate both the grace of God and the glory of God to those around us. Will we demonstrate Jesus to those who cross our paths?

Will we forgive those who've sinned against us, just as we have been forgiven?

Will we resist the temptation to judge those whose sins are different from our own?

Will we live in such a way that his glory is seen in our lives?

Will we reach out to those around us who are struggling to let them know of a better life in Jesus Christ?

While we wait, we have a chance to dive deeply into God's grace and reflect his glory.

Amen.

Nativity of the Lord Proper II
Titus 3:4-7

Rebirth And Renewal

> *But when the goodness and loving kindness of God our Savior appeared, he saved us, not because of any works of righteousness that we had done, but according to his mercy, through the water of rebirth and renewal by the Holy Spirit. This Spirit he poured out on us richly through Jesus Christ our Savior, so that, having been justified by his grace, we might become heirs according to the hope of eternal life.*

Rebirth and renewal: the words inspire hope and encouragement. There is a sense of freshness or newness connected with those words. The coming of Jesus and his kingdom provide those who have a relationship with him with a chance to begin again.

There is something liberating about getting a chance to start over. I remember a time when that mattered to me. I was in the second grade at Muncie Elementary School in Kansas City. It was near Christmas and our teacher gave us a coloring sheet with a reindeer on it. As a second grader, I was interested in more things than just reindeer. I quickly colored the reindeer, and then turned the page over to draw what I really liked. I drew tanks and soldiers. I filled the back of the page. Pretty soon the battle spilled over to the front, too. I was so engrossed in my drawing that I didn't notice the teacher was putting our reindeer on the bulletin board. My reindeer was surrounded by a battle. There was no way I wanted that up on the board. I didn't know she was going to hang them up. I awkwardly got out of my seat and asked if I might have another reindeer sheet. I still remember how relieved I was that she gave me one. She gave me another chance.

Getting another chance; that's the message for fallen humanity. We see this clearly in this short passage from Titus. This passage is one long sentence in the Greek language, and it provides us a powerful reminder of what Jesus' kingdom is to be. The build up to Christmas Day is a busy time. There is so much to do, and so many places to go. Once

Christmas Day arrives, our thoughts can turn all too quickly to cleaning up after the festivities and going back to the daily grind. Beyond a gathering of family, parties, meals, and presents, what difference does Christmas make in the real world? Paul answered that for us.

God's Kindness Is Displayed

The first thing we see is God's kindness is prominent in the celebration of Christmas. Verse four says, "But when the goodness and loving kindness of God our Savior appeared." A word study of this verse reveals some fascinating things. The word for "goodness" and "loving kindness" involves more than warm and fuzzy feelings. People who are truly kind will reach out to help a person in need. The word for "loving" is speaking of "loving people" (*phileo*). That's what is happening here. God is showing his love for people. How? The Savior appeared. This is the word from which the English word "epiphany" derives. It means literally, "to shine a light on" or "make appear." Jesus is the physical manifestation of the loving kindness of God.

There is something profoundly moving about kindness. A story is told about Abraham Lincoln that depicts kindness. The story is unverified but fits the character of the sixteenth president.

Despite his busy schedule during the Civil War, Abraham Lincoln visited the hospitals to cheer the wounded. On one occasion he saw a young man who was near death. "Is there anything I can do for you?" asked the compassionate President. "Please write a letter to my mother," came the reply. Unrecognized by the soldier, the President sat down and wrote as the youth told him what to say. As he concluded the letter, he wrote, "Written for your son by Abraham Lincoln."

When given the letter to read, the soldier was astonished to discover who had shown him such kindness. "Are you really the president?" he asked. "Yes," was the quiet answer. "Now, is there anything else I can do?" The lad feebly replied, "Will you please hold my hand? I think it would help to see me through to the end." Lincoln granted his request, offering words of encouragement until death stole in with the dawn.

God has even more than that. God has provided us, in his loving kindness, a way to escape the finality of death. Jesus, the physical representation of his kindness, came to bring life and usher us into his glorious kingdom.

Renewal And Rebirth

Verse seven notes, "he saved us, not because of any works of righteousness that we had done, but according to his mercy, through the water of rebirth and renewal by the Holy Spirit." Christians experience the loving kindness of God through the waters of renewal and rebirth. The Holy Spirit engages us in the waters of baptism. The word for renewal is the Greek word *anakainosis*. That word is a combination of *ana* (again) and *kainoo* (to make qualitatively new — fundamentally new). Literally, this word is "to make fundamentally new again."

It is unusual to consider baptism with the Christmas message, but according to this text there is a connection between Jesus' incarnation and our regeneration. Because he came, we can be transformed. Part of the process of that transformation is baptism. Through God's grace and by no works of our own, we can enter his kingdom. Part of that entering is the wonderful experience of being baptized into Christ and being renewed by the Holy Spirit.

College football fans will recognize the name Bill McCartney. McCartney was the successful coach of the Colorado Buffaloes football team. He led the Buffs to a national championship and multiple bowl games. He retired at the height of his success after the 1994 season. McCartney said that he was retiring because he wanted to reevaluate his priorities. He was convinced he needed to be a better husband and better follower of Jesus. That renewal led him to start the group that became Promise Keepers.

Renewal and rebirth are vital for us. What will that look like for you? It may not mean you start a new, nation-wide movement, but it may mean you are different. You are not the same husband, wife, father, mother, worker, boss, leader, student, man, or woman you were before. God desires to use all of us for his kingdom's sake. Through the coming of Jesus and our renewal and rebirth, we can be used for his glory. What will that look like for you?

Glorious Inheritance

This results in us becoming heirs of his kingdom through the amazing grace of God. Is there any greater gift for us than that? Through Jesus Christ, we are recipients of something far greater than we can even imagine. An heir is a person who has the legal right to an inheritance.

Jewish law regulated inheritances, giving two shares to the firstborn son and one share each to the other sons (Deuteronomy 21:17). Paul is reiterating that those who have a relationship with Jesus will inherit eternal life, spending forever with God.

On this Christmas Day, may we be mindful that because of his first advent, we can become a part of God's family. We can have the rights of sons and receive a gift far greater than any that we find under our tree. May we humbly receive that gift this Christmas.

Amen.

Nativity of the Lord-Proper III
Hebrews 1:1-4, (5-12)

Superior To All

Long ago God spoke to our ancestors in many and various ways by the prophets, but in these last days he has spoken to us by a Son, whom he appointed heir of all things, through whom he also created the worlds. He is the reflection of God's glory and the exact imprint of God's very being, and he sustains all things by his powerful word. When he had made purification for sins, he sat down at the right hand of the Majesty on high, having become as much superior to angels as the name he has inherited is more excellent than theirs.

A seminary student wrote of an incident that happened while he was in school. Since the school they attended had no gym, the guys played basketball in a nearby public school. Whenever they played an elderly janitor waited patiently until they were finished. Often, he read his Bible while waiting. One day one of the young men asked him what he was reading. The man answered, 'The book of Revelation.' Surprised, the seminary student asked if he understood it. 'Oh, yes,' the man assured him. `I understand it.' 'What does it mean?' Quietly the janitor answered, "It means that Jesus is going to win."

Is there any better summary than that? Is there any more important truth than the fact that Jesus is going to win? In the text today, we find powerful and significant descriptions of Jesus, whose first arrival we celebrate, and whose second arrival we anticipate. The Hebrew writer begins by noting how God has communicated previously. He did so through the word of prophets. Now, though, things have changed. The message of God's kingdom is delivered by the Son of God, himself. Then, the writer of Hebrews gives us a glimpse of who Jesus is. These descriptions reverberate with power.

Heir And Creator Of All Things
The first is that he is the "heir of all things" and the one through whom God created the worlds. Jesus is the one who has authority over all things as he is the heir of the kingdom. He is also the one who created all that is. The whole creation, visible and invisible, was made for him, as well as by him (Colossians 1:16). This characterization of Jesus gives us a glimpse of his greatness and power.

On New Year's Day, the Tournament of Roses parade is held in Pasadena, California. One particular year, a beautiful float suddenly sputtered and quit. It was out of gas. The whole parade was held up until someone could get a can of gas. The ironic thing was this float represented the Standard Oil Company. With its vast oil resources, its float was out of gas.

That is something we do not have to be concerned about with Jesus. He created all things; all things were made for him, and he has the power and authority to rule. He will not stumble or fall as others might. There is nothing too great for him.

A tragic prognosis is not the end for the one who knows Jesus. It may well be the beginning of something far greater than ever imagined.

Disasters and calamities in this world do not have to devastate the child of God. Jesus can use them to demonstrate his incredible grace and power.

Broken homes and relationships do not have to weigh down the one who knows Jesus as Lord. He may use it as a way for you to glorify him.

Who he is and the fact of his coming means life can be made new. Nothing that happens to us in this life must define us. Jesus is greater than all of that.

Reflection Of God's Glory And The Exact Imprint Of His Being
These two descriptions are wonderfully rich. Jesus is the "reflection of God's glory." The word here implies a beam of sunlight that emanates from the sun, itself. That is how Jesus is. He is the glory of God. The second, "the exact imprint of his being" implies the coin a king would use to put his seal upon a letter or document. The imprint of the seal is exactly what is on it. That's how Jesus is with God. These two descriptions exclaim exactly who Jesus is. He is God.

What does that mean? Jesus is not a god. He is not a good teacher and like God. He *is* God. There is power and authority in that declaration. Walter Ewell wrote of the incarnation: Jesus as fully God and fully man. He noted the word was "Literally, "en-flesh-ment" (Latin *carnis* "flesh"); the doctrine that the Son of God became human (John 1:14). Jesus did not play at becoming a man but took on our flesh with all its problems and weaknesses. Incarnation, in the Christian understanding, means that Christ was both God and human."[13]

Our Christmas celebration is truly about "Emmanuel." Literally, God is with us. We do not worship a God who is far removed from us and unaware of what it means to be human. "For we do not have a high priest who is unable to empathize with our weaknesses, but we have one who has been tempted in every way, just as we are — yet he did not sin" (Hebrews 4:15).

Savior: Made Purification For Our Sins

The final description here is one of Jesus as the Savior. He "made purification for sins and sat down at the right hand of the majesty on high." This description of Jesus is one with which we are familiar. He is the Savior, the sacrifice, the one who gives his life for fallen humanity. He paid the price for sin, once and for all. The debt we owed has been paid. Now, he takes his place of power and authority at the right hand of the Father.

The word "Savior" is a powerful word. It stimulates images of powerful leaders who crash the scene and bring deliverance and hope to a downtrodden people.

NBA fans know that Michael Jordan was regarded as the "savior" of the Chicago Bulls franchise. The Bulls had no championships before Jordan, and six during his career. However, his ability to affect long-term change was limited. The Bulls have had no championships since his retirement.

Marvel Comic book fans know all about the Avengers. They are often heroes and saviors to a desperate world. The Avengers, though, are fictional. Their adventures, while fascinating on the screen, have no real impact. They are fantasy saviors.

Sports saviors and fantasy saviors have a definite appeal, but, ultimately, they fall short of being meaningful. Only one Savior stands the test of time. Only one Savior has done something that carries eternal

---

13 Walter A. Elwell, *The Shaw Pocket Bible Handbook*, (Wheaton IL: Harold Shaw Publishing, 1984), 351.

significance. Only one Savior really matters. Do you know that Savior? This Christmas we celebrate the coming of the one who paid our debt, and we long for his return to take us to glory.

Amen.

First Sunday After Christmas Day
Galatians 4:4-7

We Are Family

> *But when the fullness of time had come, God sent his Son, born of a woman, born under the law, in order to redeem those who were under the law, so that we might receive adoption as children. And because you are children, God has sent the Spirit of his Son into our hearts, crying, "Abba! Father!" So you are no longer a slave but a child, and if a child then also an heir through God.*

On June 1, 1979, the Pittsburgh Pirates' game against the Padres was delayed as rain pounded the Three Rivers Stadium turf. The Pirates were a team loaded with all-stars but was struggling. During the rain delay, Willie Stargell, the leader of the team, made a decision that would affect the whole season. While the players chatted in the dugout, waiting for the game to get underway, Sister Sledge's "We Are Family," the number four hit song that week — blared over the speakers.

Stargell called the press box with a strange request. "Joe, when this song is done," Stargell said to the Pirates PR Director Joe Safety, "I want you to make the announcement that this is the official Pirates clubhouse song." It was a huge hit that June day and became a catalyst for the Pirates World Series Championship.[14]

"We Are Family." It was an engaging song over four decades ago, and its message still resonates. In many ways, it is what Paul is reminding the Galatian Christians of in this passage. A week removed from Christmas; it is a good reminder for us today.

The Christmas story is briefly recounted in verse four. God's sending of his Son ends the reign of the law and inaugurates a new age. The Son is "born of a woman." This indicates that he is fully human. He is a man in every way. He is also "born under the law." This seems to put Jesus in the center of human experience (Hebrews 4:15). His purpose

---

[14] Michael Clair, "How the Pirates chose 'We Are Family' in '79: Sister Sledge helped lead the Pirates to a World Series," *MLB*, February 18, 2022, https://www.mlb.com/news/how-the-pirates-chose-we-are-family-as-their-anthem

in coming is stated in verse five. That purpose and the result form an incredible message.

Redeemed

Verse five notes the reason Jesus came. He came "in order to redeem those under the law." The word "redeem" literally means "to buy back." The image Paul paints is clear. Prior to Jesus, human beings were enslaved to sin. The law points out where humanity falls short (Romans 3:19-20). We also know that "the wages of sin is death" (Romans 3:23). Jesus redeems lost and captive people. He buys them back.

John Newton's story is well-known. He wrote the famous hymn, *Amazing Grace*. Books and movies have chronicled his life. He was an only child whose mother died when he was seven years old. He became a sailor and went out to sea at eleven years old. As he grew up, he became the captain of a slave ship. Late in his life, he became a Christian. The thoughtful words of *Amazing Grace* take on deeper meaning understanding from whose pen they flowed. What may not be as well-known is what Newton had painted above his fireplace. Words from Isaiah 43:4 and Deuteronomy 15:15 — "Since thou were precious in my sight, thou hast been honorable — *but* — thou shalt remember that thou were a bond-man in the land of Egypt, and the Lord thy God redeemed thee."[15]

Newton wanted to remember he had been redeemed. May we, too, never forget.

Receive Adoption

The result of redemption is that lost humanity can be adopted into God's family. In this passage, Paul likely has in mind the Roman custom of adoption, in which adopted sons were given equal privileges in the family and equal status as heirs.[16] We who were once separated from God have not only been bought back, but we have been given family status. It is the epitome of the Prodigal Son story (Luke 15). We can be a part of the family of God.

Belonging to a family is important. One of the most inspirational adoption stories is that of Michael Oher. Oher was seventeen years old when Sean and Leigh Ann Tuohy adopted him. Oher joined the

---

15 David B. Calhoun, "Amazing Grace: John Newton and his Great Hymn, *C.S. Lewis Institute*, December 1, 2013. https://www.cslewisinstitute.org/resources/amazing-grace-john-newton-and-his-great-hymn/

16 Carol Ashby, "Adoption in the Roman Empire," https://carolashby.com/adoption-in-the-roman-empire/

Tuohy's other two children and, while it was not a perfect life, it was a good life. Oher was drafted by the Baltimore Ravens and was part of their 2013 Super Bowl championship team. The 2009 movie *The Blindside* depicted this family relationship. It was clear from Michael Oher's story, belonging matters.[17]

You, too, can belong. It does not matter where you have been or what you have done. God offers to bring you into his family. The relationship described in this passage is an intimate one. Verse six notes, "God has sent the Spirit of his Son into our hearts, crying, "Abba! Father!" The word "Abba" is a revealing one. Many times, we have translated this word, "Daddy," to demonstrate the close intimacy we have with God. Chad Harrington contends that definition is partially right. The term "Abba" does show intimacy. Harrington also argues that the word also implies "obedience" or "respect."[18] Our adoption gives us both the *right* and the *ability* to cry out "Daddy!" to God our Father, even as Jesus did. Through our adoption, we are afforded a wonderful chance to interact with God.

Interactions with your father matter. Charles Francis Adams, son of President John Quincy Adams and grandson of President John Adams, kept a diary. One day he entered: "Went fishing with my son today — a day wasted." His son, Brook Adams, also kept a diary, which is still in existence. On that same day, Brook Adams made this entry: "Went fishing with my father — the most wonderful day of my life!" The father thought he was wasting time while fishing with his son, but his son saw it as an investment of time.[19]

God never sees it that way. Earthly fathers can fail and not do what they ought to do. God is not like that. He will be consistent, loving, and nurturing. He will not let you down. God has made it possible for you to be in his family. He wants to be your father. That's the point of what we just celebrated at Christmas. You can be in the family of the king.

Amen.

---

17 Joshua Rogers, "Michael Oher's relationship with the Tuohy family in 2022 Explored," *The Focus*, March 2022, https://www.thefocus.news/sports/nfl/is-michael-oher-still-close-to-the-tuohy-family-in-2022/

18 Chad Harrington, "The Biblical Meaning of 'Abba,' and It's Not Daddy," About Him Publications, https://himpublications.com/blog/meaning-abba/

19 Rick Johnson, *Better Dads, Stronger Sons* Ada, MI: Fleming H. Revell Publishing, 2006, 78.

Baptism of the Lord
Acts 19:1-7

Entering The Kingdom

> *While Apollos was in Corinth, Paul passed through the interior regions and came to Ephesus, where he found some disciples. He said to them, "Did you receive the Holy Spirit when you became believers?" They replied, "No, we have not even heard that there is a Holy Spirit." Then he said, "Into what, then, were you baptized?" They answered, "Into John's baptism." Paul said, "John baptized with the baptism of repentance, telling the people to believe in the one who was to come after him, that is, in Jesus." On hearing this, they were baptized in the name of the Lord Jesus. When Paul had laid his hands on them, the Holy Spirit came upon them, and they spoke in tongues and prophesied, altogether there were about twelve of them.*

As a child, I liked the movie *Willy Wonka and the Chocolate Factory* that featured Gene Wilder as the candy-maker Wonka. The movie is based loosely on the 1964 book by Roald Dahl. The movie is about how five children got to visit Wonka's secret candy factory. There were lots of interesting and unusual things in that movie, including the "oompa loompas." Entrance into this wonderful, strange chocolate factory was dependent on a "golden ticket" that opened the door.

What opens the door to the kingdom of God? We've been looking at this kingdom and anticipating Jesus' return. In this text, we find an important component of our entrance into his kingdom. As this text begins, Paul is on his third missionary journey. He has traveled through Asia Minor, visiting churches he started earlier. He is now at the beginning of what will be about a three-year preaching ministry in Ephesus. Apollos has also ministered in Ephesus. His story is told in Acts 18:24-28. It is important to note that in Acts 18:25 it says of Apollos that he "taught about Jesus accurately, though he knew only the baptism of John." Priscilla and Aquila heard him speak and invited him to their home, where they instructed him more completely about the "way of God" undoubtedly including baptism. There is a distinction between the baptism of repentance and baptism in Jesus. Baptism is the culminating act of faith for one who wants to enter the kingdom of God. There are some important truths that we ought to see about baptism and the kingdom.

Baptism Is An Identifying Act

Being baptized into Jesus Christ identifies us with Jesus. "Therefore, we were buried with him by baptism into death, so that, just as Christ was raised from the dead by the glory of the Father, so we also might walk in newness of life" (Romans 6:4). When we are baptized, we are declaring to the world a desire to be connected to Jesus. In a discussion with Nicodemus, Jesus said, "Very truly, I tell you, no one can enter the kingdom of God without being born of water and Spirit" (John 3:5).

Being like Jesus makes a difference. I read about a group of salesmen who went to a sales convention in Chicago. They told their wives that they would be home in plenty of time for dinner. In their rush through the airport, one of the salesmen accidentally kicked over a table which held a basket of apples. Apples flew everywhere. Without stopping or looking back, they all managed to reach the plane, just in time. All but one. He told the others to go on without him and went back to where the apples were all over the floor. The one selling the apples was a blind girl. She was softly crying, tears running down her cheeks, as she groped for her spilled produce. The crowd swirled around her, rushing to their flights. No one paid any attention.

The salesman, however, knelt on the floor with her, gathered up the apples, put them back on the table and helped reorganize her display. He set aside the bruised and battered apples in a separate basket. When he had finished, he pulled out his wallet and said to the girl, "Here, please take this $40 for the damage we did."

"Are you okay?" he asked her. She nodded through her tears. He continued, "I hope we didn't spoil your day too badly."

As the salesman started to walk away, the bewildered blind girl called out to him, "Mister," and he paused and turned, "Are you Jesus?"

That question echoes in our minds. Identifying with Jesus matters. Baptism is the initial way we identify with him. "As many of you as were baptized into Christ have clothed yourselves with Christ" (Galatians 3:27).

Baptism As A Transformative Act

Baptism is also a transformative act acknowledging cleansing from sin and the indwelling of the Holy Spirit. Paul, describing his own conversion, notes what Ananias told him. "And now why do you delay? Get up, be baptized, and have your sins washed away, calling on his name" (Acts 22:16).

Baptism relates to the forgiveness of sins and being made new. Paul wrote, "when you were buried with him in baptism, you were also raised with him through faith in the power of God, who raised him from the dead. And when you were dead in trespasses and the uncircumcision of your flesh, God made you alive together with him, when he forgave us all our trespasses" (Colossians 2:12-13). Baptism represents that new birth. Our old way of life is gone and the new emerges.

Transformation is a beautiful sight. L.B.E. Cowman shared this story in her book, *Springs in the Valley*.

> Sir Edwin Landseer was one of the most famous painters of the Victorian era. His talent developed early, and he had the first showing of his work at the Royal Academy when he was just thirteen years old. He was commissioned to do a number of official portraits of the royal family, and even gave private drawing lessons to Queen Victoria and Prince Albert. But he was best known for his depictions of the natural settings and life in the Scottish Highlands.
>
> One day as he was visiting a family in an old mansion in Scotland, one of the servants spilled a pitcher of soda water, leaving a large stain on the wall. While the family was out for the day, Landseer remained behind. Using charcoal, he incorporated the stain into a beautiful drawing. When the family returned, they found a picture of a waterfall surrounded by trees and animals. He used his skill to make something beautiful out of what had been an unsightly mess.[20]

Making something beautiful out of an unsightly mess. Sir Edwin Landseer, a remarkable artist, did that with a wall. Jesus Christ does that, too, with something far more valuable than a wall. He can make something beautiful of a messed-up life. Baptism acknowledges that incredible change.

Amen.

---

[20] L.B.E. Cowman, *Springs in the Valley*, (Grand Rapids, MI: Zondervan Publishing Company, 1997), 116.

Second Sunday after the Epiphany
1 Corinthians 6:12-20

Prepare Our Bodies For The Kingdom

"All things are permitted for me," but not all things are beneficial. "All things are permitted for me," but I will not be dominated by anything. "Food is meant for the stomach and the stomach for food," and God will destroy both one and the other. The body is meant not for sexual immorality but for the Lord and the Lord for the body. And God raised the Lord and will also raise us by his power. Do you not know that your bodies are members of Christ? Should I therefore take the members of Christ and make them members of a prostitute? Never! Do you not know that whoever is united to a prostitute becomes one body with her? For it is said, "The two shall be one flesh." But anyone united to the Lord becomes one spirit with him. Shun sexual immorality! Every sin that a person commits is outside the body, but the sexually immoral person sins against the body itself. Or do you not know that your body is a temple of the Holy Spirit within you, which you have from God, and that you are not your own? For you were bought with a price; therefore, glorify God in your body.

On December 2, 2012, Spanish athlete Iván Fernández Anaya was competing in a cross-country race in Burlada, Navarre. He was running second, some distance behind race leader Abel Mutai — bronze medalist in the 3,000-meter steeplechase at the London Olympics. As they entered the finishing straight, he saw the Kenyan runner — the certain winner of the race — mistakenly pull up about ten meters before the finish, thinking he had already crossed the line.

Fernández Anaya quickly caught up with him, but instead of exploiting Mutai's mistake to speed past and claim an unlikely victory, he stayed behind and, using gestures, guided the Kenyan to the line and let him cross first.

"I didn't deserve to win it," says 24-year-old Fernández Anaya. "I did what I had to do. He was the rightful winner. He created a gap that

I couldn't have closed if he hadn't made a mistake. As soon as I saw he was stopping, I knew I wasn't going to pass him."[21]

Self-sacrifice is unusual, in the world of sports and beyond. It is, however, the way of the kingdom of God. Paul highlights that kingdom principle in 1 Corinthians 6. There are two themes that emerge from this text that underscore how a citizen of God's kingdom is selfless.

Use Your Freedom Well

Becoming a Christian is about being set free from the heavy chains of sin. Despite what some might assert, the Christian faith is not a list of what you can and cannot do. There is freedom in being a follower of Jesus. Paul makes it clear, though, that this freedom is not a license to sin (Romans 6:1-2). He also notes that we have a responsibility to use our freedom well. Just because we can do something doesn't mean we should. Paul wrote, "All things are permitted for me," but not all things are beneficial. All things are permitted for me, but I will not be dominated by anything" (v. 12). A citizen of God's kingdom exercises self-control and is mindful of his witness.

I am a fan of American history and did a bit of research on the original thirteen colonies. Many people are not aware that the original seal of the state of Georgia has a mulberry leaf, a silkworm, and a cocoon. The seal also had the Latin phrase *sibi sed allis*, not for us but for others. The colony of Georgia was founded a bit differently than the others.

James Oglethorpe was the founder of the Georgia colony. His goal was to start a charity colony in America. On June 9, 1732, the king granted a charter to the Trustees for Establishing the Colony of Georgia. Oglethorpe himself led the first group of 114 colonists on the frigate *Anne*, landing at the site of today's Savannah on February 1, 1733. The original charter banned slavery and granted religious freedom, leading to the foundation of a Jewish community in Savannah.[22] Oglethorpe was also inspired to create a colony to give the poor a chance to succeed as farmers, merchants, and artisans.

Putting others first was James Oglethorpe's passion. Is it ours?

---

21 Carlos Arribas, "Honesty of the Long-Distance Runner," International Fair Play Journal, December 19, 2012, http://www.fairplayinternational.org/honesty-of-the-long-distance-runner

22 "James Edward Oglethorpe," https://oglethorpe.edu/about/history-traditions/james-edward-oglethorpe/

God Paid A High Price For You: Live Like It

"You were bought at a price. You are not your own" (v. 20). These are hard words to hear in today's culture. We like the idea of being our own boss and controlling our own destiny. Part of the selfishness of this culture is expressed in "I Did It My Way."

Timothy McVeigh's last words before his execution were a quote from William Ernest Henley's poem, "Invictus." His final words were, "It matters not how strait the gate. How charged with punishments the scroll, I am the master of my fate: I am the captain of my soul."[23] It seems for McVeigh, it was all about himself.

The truth is Christians are not the captain of their souls. We have been bought at a price. What was that price? Jesus' life. The chorus of Elvina M. Hall's hymn, "Jesus Paid It All," says:

> Jesus paid it all,
> All to Him I owe;
> Sin had left a crimson stain,
> He washed it white as snow.[24]

The warning here is about sexual immorality. The Lord wants his people to be pure and clean. We should not allow ourselves to be marred by the things of the world.

At one time I collected baseball cards. I still have quite a few. While some of them are in rough shape, I have several that are in excellent to mint condition and are worth some money. Whenever I buy a card from another dealer, I want to check the condition. Any card collector would. The reason is obvious. You must make sure that what you are spending a lot of money for is in the most valuable condition. A torn or damaged card is just not worth the price.

Jesus doesn't see things the way a card collector does. He was willing to pay the price for the damaged, broken, torn, and messed up cards. Our response, though, is important. Since such a price was paid for us, what kind of lives will we live? Will we allow that which cost Jesus so much to be stained and tainted by that which matters so little?

God paid a high price for you: live like it.

Amen.

---

23 "McVeigh's Final Statement," The Guardian, June 11, 2001, https://www.theguardian.com/world/2001/jun/11/mcveigh.usa1

24 Elvina M. Hall, "Jesus Paid It All," Hymnary, https://hymnary.org/text/i_hear_the_savior_say_thy_strength_indee In the public domain.

Third Sunday after the Epiphany
1 Corinthians 7:29-31

The Time Is Short

> *I mean, brothers and sisters, the appointed time has grown short; from now on, let even those who have wives be as though they had none, and those who mourn as though they were not mourning, and those who rejoice as though they were not rejoicing, and those who buy as though they had no possessions, and those who deal with the world as though they had no dealings with it. For the present form of this world is passing away.*

A little girl was having trouble sleeping at night. A few different times she called out to her mom and dad. She wanted a drink. She had to go to the bathroom. Could she hear another story? Her comments seemed endless. Her exasperated parents finally told her it was late, and she could not call out to them again. She whimpered a bit but nodded. Still, she could not fall asleep. She listened to the grandfather clock in the hallway chime. First, she heard ten chimes. Then she heard eleven. The clock malfunctioned at midnight, however, and it chimed and chimed and chimed. Her parents stepped out, so she did, too. The clock continued to chime. She looked to her father and said, "Wow, Daddy. It's later than ever!"

"It's later than ever." That might have been an accurate description of what happened to that grandfather clock, and it is a good summary of what Paul was writing. Paul was writing about the kingdom of God in apocalyptic terms. For Christians, a relationship with Jesus Christ means salvation (present and future) and reconciliation to God. It also gives us a moral foundation from which to view the world. Paul notes, too, that Jesus' birth, death, and resurrection inaugurates the end. Paul was convinced that, now that Christ has come and has displayed perfect obedience in his death, the end was very near. We celebrate the coming of the King of kings. We understand that we are invited to be a part of this glorious kingdom. We know that it exists, in part now, as the Holy Spirit indwells all Christians. We should also understand that our time here is short. Recognition of that should influence how we live.

Don't Be Distracted

In this passage, Paul urged the Christians in Corinth to not be distracted by the lesser things of this world. It isn't that these things are inherently bad. The point is that something far greater is imminent on the horizon. Jesus will be coming back. Paul was certain of this truth, and we can be, too. If his return was imminent in Paul's day, how much closer is it today? We ought to live with his return in mind. It's easy, though, to get distracted.

J.M. Boice wrote,

> There is a story involving Yogi Berra, the well-known catcher for the New York Yankees, and Hank Aaron, who at that time was the chief power hitter for the Milwaukee Braves. The teams were playing in the World Series, and as usual Yogi was keeping up his ceaseless chatter, intended to pep up his teammates on the one hand, and distract the Milwaukee batters on the other. As Aaron came to the plate, Yogi tried to distract him by saying, "Henry, you're holding the bat wrong. You're supposed to hold it so you can read the trademark." Aaron didn't say anything, but when the next pitch came, he hit it into the left-field bleachers. After rounding the bases and tagging up at home plate, Aaron looked at Yogi Berra and said, "I didn't come up here to read."[25]

Hank Aaron refused to be distracted by the gregarious Berra. Will we maintain the same focus? The lures of this world are tempting.

"There's plenty of time to do that Christian stuff. Have fun for a while."

"You can tell her about Jesus next month. There's no rush."

"Live a little. You can always repent later."

"Make some money first and then consider helping others."

"You'd better take care of you. You are the most important person you know."

As we step up to the plate, Satan chirps these lies to us. His goal was the same as Berra's. He wants us to lose focus. Take our eyes off

---

25 J.M. Boice, *Nehemiah, Learning to Lead*, (Grand Rapids, MI: Revell Books, 1990), 38.

the ball. Will we display the intense focus of Hammering Hank? What did we come up to the plate to do?

Focus Intensely

Paul challenged the Corinthian Christians to be focused on what matters. Live as if you had no spouse, possessions, and worldly engagements. His reason was clear. "The present form of this world is passing away" (1 Corinthians 7:31). Paul expected the imminent arrival of Christ in his glory, and that makes a difference as to how one should live. Focus matters.

Carol Mann shared this story in her book *The 19th Hole: Favorite Golf Stories*.

> Golf immortal Arnold Palmer recalls a lesson about overconfidence: It was the final hole of the 1961 Masters tournament, and I had a one-stroke lead and had just hit a very satisfying tee shot. I felt I was in pretty good shape. As I approached my ball, I saw an old friend standing at the edge of the gallery. He motioned me over, stuck out his hand and said, "Congratulations." I took his hand and shook it, but as soon as I did, I knew I had lost my focus.
>
> On my next two shots, I hit the ball into a sand trap, then put it over the edge of the green. I missed a putt and lost the Masters. You don't forget a mistake like that; you just learn from it and become determined that you will never do that again. I haven't in the thirty years since.[26]

Losing focus cost one of the world's greatest golfers the Masters Championship. Losing focus in life can be even more devastating. Jesus is coming back. We celebrated his first coming with the clear expectation he will return. Are we focused on living the life we are called to live or are we just having a good time? There is nothing wrong with enjoying the life God gives us, but we should not lose sight of his promised return.

Are you mindful of your witness and willing to share your love of Jesus with those around you?

Are you seeking to become more like Jesus each day, or seeing how far from him you can walk and still be considered "Christian?"

---

26 Carol Mann, *The 19th Hole: Favorite Golf Stories*, (Ann Arbor, MI: Longmeadow Books, 1992), 46.

Are you and your family standing up for what is right and biblical, or do you just do what everyone else does?

Keeping focus is not an easy task, but it matters.

Amen.

Fourth Sunday after the Epiphany
1 Corinthians 8:1-13

Sacrifice For The Kingdom's Sake

> *Now concerning food sacrificed to idols: we know that "all of us possess knowledge." Knowledge puffs up, but love builds up. Anyone who claims to know something does not yet have the necessary knowledge, but anyone who loves God is known by him.*
>
> *Hence, as to the eating of food offered to idols, we know that "no idol in the world really exists" and that "there is no God but one." Indeed, even though there may be so-called gods in heaven or on earth — as in fact there are many gods and many lords — yet for us there is one God, the Father, from whom are all things and for whom we exist, and one Lord, Jesus Christ, through whom are all things and through whom we exist.*
>
> *It is not everyone, however, who has this knowledge. Since some have become so accustomed to idols until now, they still think of the food they eat as food offered to an idol, and their conscience, being weak, is defiled. "Food will not bring us close to God." We are no worse off if we do not eat and no better off if we do. But take care that this liberty of yours does not somehow become a stumbling block to the weak. For if others see you, who possess knowledge, eating in the temple of an idol, might they not, since their conscience is weak, be encouraged to the point of eating food sacrificed to idols? So by your knowledge the weak brother or sister for whom Christ died is destroyed. But when you thus sin against brothers and sisters and wound their conscience when it is weak, you sin against Christ. Therefore, if food is a cause of their falling, I will never again eat meat, so that I may not cause one of them to fall.*

There are many wonderful blessings for us in the kingdom of God. We are free to do all kinds of things. Kingdom citizenship, however, comes with responsibility. A citizen of God's kingdom understands self-sacrifice. Paul wrote about a self-giving love modeled on God's own love, demonstrated in the giving of his Son. It is a love not based on the worthiness of the other person but is given anyway. Love such as this, Paul said, builds up the community.

In this passage, Paul challenged his readers and us to be willing to sacrifice for the kingdom's sake. That idea is highlighted by two specific points.

Choose Love Over Spiritual Arrogance
Paul wrote in verse 1, "Now concerning food sacrificed to idols: we know that 'all of us possess knowledge.' Knowledge puffs up, but love builds up." Paul is making an interesting contrast. The "knowledge" he references here is not just an understanding of things. He is describing a spiritual sophistication that borders on spiritual arrogance. Paul acknowledges that they know they have freedom in Christ. That kind of knowledge, unchecked by love, leads to arrogance and an "I can do what I want attitude." The challenge is to replace that attitude with love.

Michael Haskew shares this story. During the Battle of Spotsylvania in the Civil War, Union general John Sedgwick was inspecting his troops. At one point he came to a parapet, over which he gazed out in the direction of the enemy. His officers suggested that this was unwise and perhaps he ought to duck while passing the parapet. "Nonsense," snapped the general. "They couldn't hit an elephant at this distance." As the words left his mouth, Sedgwick fell to the ground, mortally wounded.[27]

Arrogance can lead to bad situations. Spiritual arrogance can be even more deadly. Note the contrasts. The spiritually arrogant focus on self. Those who love focus on others. The spiritually arrogant demand to do what they want to do. Those who choose love do what helps others and pleases God. The spiritually arrogant are enamored with how right they are. Christians who choose love believe there is no one righteous but the Lord. The spiritually arrogant are impressed by their own lives. Spiritual arrogance puffs up with no inherent value. Love is what builds up. Choose to love. Choose to focus on your brother.

Choose Your Brother Over Your Freedom
Paul wrote, "But take care that this liberty of yours does not somehow become a stumbling block to the weak" (v.9). Paul's admonition is to look out for your brother. Do not do anything, even if it is permissible,

---

27 Michael E. Haskew, *The Sniper at War*, (Cheltenham, Gloucestershire, UK: Spellmount Publishers, 2004), 102.

that might cause your brother or sister to sin. This is how a citizen of God's kingdom thinks and acts. It is the embodiment of what Jesus said about the second greatest commandment, "'Love your neighbor as yourself" (Mark 12:31). A citizen of God's kingdom is concerned for his brother or sister.

In Suzanne Collins' book, *The Hunger Games*, the Capital rules over the twelve districts of Panem. Every year a lottery was held to choose two tributes from each district to compete in "the hunger games," a reality TV competition where the tributes fight to the death. Katniss Everdeen's worst nightmare came true when her little sister Prim was randomly selected to be a tribute. Katniss is repulsed by the idea of Prim in the "Hunger Games," so she volunteered to go in her place.

Katniss displayed selflessness. That's what Paul was exhorting Christians to show. It is not about what you can do, it is about what is the best thing for you to do with respect to others.

You can have one drink with dinner, but would you if you were eating with an alcoholic?

You can watch that movie, but should you if you are with someone who struggles with lust?

You can have a couples' date night, but is it the best choice if one member of your group is recently divorced?

You can binge watch that television show, but should you if the person you are with is tempted to dabble in the occult?

Christians have been set free. However, we are not to use that freedom to cause a brother or sister to stumble. Will you be a steppingstone or a stumbling block? We are citizens of God's kingdom. Part of who we are is that, like Jesus, we put others ahead of ourselves. Though we know that we have freedom, that freedom is not more important than the people around us.

Amen.

Presentation of the Lord
Hebrews 2:14-18

He Became One Of Us

Since, therefore, the children share flesh and blood, he himself likewise shared the same things, so that through death he might destroy the one who has the power of death, that is, the devil, and free those who all their lives were held in slavery by the fear of death. For it is clear that he did not come to help angels but the descendants of Abraham. Therefore he had to become like his brothers and sisters in every respect, so that he might become a merciful and faithful high priest in the service of God, to make a sacrifice of atonement for the sins of the people. Because he himself was tested by what he suffered; he is able to help those who are being tested.

The incarnation of Jesus is one of the most important and discussed theological concepts. Clearly, it is impossible for humanity to redeem itself. "There is no one righteous, not even one" (Romans 3:10). Only the blood of a perfect, sinless man will be sufficient to save a guilty race. Only the death of a kinsman can redeem lost humanity. This is the impetus behind the incarnation.

C.S. Lewis explained the incarnation in a tangible way. Your dog is lying at your feet. Imagine, at that moment, that your dog and every dog is in deep distress. Some of us love dogs very much. If it would help all the dogs in the world to become like men, would you be willing to become a dog? Would you put down your human nature, leave your loved ones, your job, hobbies, your art, literature, your music, and choose, instead of the intimate communion with your beloved, the poor substitute of looking into the beloved's face and wagging your tail, unable to smile or speak? Christ by becoming man limited the thing which to him was the most precious thing in the world; his unhampered, unhindered communion with the Father.[28] The fact of the incarnation has implications that impact nearly every area of human life.

---

28 Glen Scrivner, "All Age Christmas Talk, Galatians 4," *Christ the Truth*, December 15, 2010.

If the incarnation is at the center of the Christian faith, it is also a scandal to many. From the gnostics to contemporary Muslims, the assertion is made that it is beneath the dignity of God to become human. Modern philosophy is also repulsed by the idea that only one human in a particular time and place could constitute the eternal God. Some Christian scholars have sought to diminish the full force of the true humanity of Christ.[29] Despite the attacks, the truth remains. Jesus Christ was God in the flesh. As such, he understands the human condition.

Struggles Of Being Human

Jesus understood what it was like to be human. He knew the pangs of hunger (Mark 11:12). He felt tired (John 4:6). He experienced betrayal and misunderstanding (Mark 6:1-6). Jesus knows what we go through in this life. He walked where we walk. John 1:14 emphatically declares, "The Word became flesh and made his dwelling among us. We have seen his glory, the glory of the one and only Son, who came from the Father, full of grace and truth."

A long time ago, Frank E. Graeff wrote the words of this famous hymn. "Does Jesus care when my heart is pained too deeply for mirth or song? Oh yes, he cares. I know he cares. His heart is touched with my grief." He understands.

Those who are familiar with presidential history will know that President Gerald R. Ford is known for never having been elected to the presidency, but assuming the role of vice president and then president at the time of Richard Nixon's resignation. He is also known for falling a lot. Ford was a college football player at Michigan and sustained a knee injury. That knee gave him trouble long after his playing days. While visiting Austria in 1975, the President's bum knee gave way, and he tumbled down the Air Force One stairs. He endured ridicule and was mocked on Saturday Night Live. I came across this story from *Today in the Word*.

When former President Gerald Ford visited Northeastern State University in Tahlequah, Oklahoma several years ago, he had breakfast with some student leaders. As one of the students stepped out of an elevator, her heel caught on the carpet, and she crashed into Ford. She repeatedly apologized as he helped her to her feet, but the former

---

29 Luke Stamps, "The Humanity of Christ," The Gospel Coalition, https://www.thegospelcoalition.org/essay/the-humanity-of-christ/

president smiled sympathetically. "Don't worry, young lady," he said. "I understand perfectly."[30]

Struggle Against Sin And Temptation

Not only does Jesus know what it is like to be a human, he knows the lure of temptation and sin. "For we do not have a high priest who is unable to sympathize with our weaknesses, but we have one who in every respect has been tested as we are, yet without sin" (Hebrews 4:15). Satan has thrown his best shots at Jesus to no avail. Jesus withstood temptation and did not sin. Jesus can help us in times of testing, too.

I heard the story of an overweight businessman who decided it was time to lose some weight. He took his new diet seriously, even changing his driving route to avoid his favorite bakery. One morning, however, he showed up at work with a gigantic coffee cake. Everyone in the office scolded him, but he smiled. "This is a special coffee cake," he explained. "I accidentally drove by the bakery this morning and there in the window was a host of goodies. I knew it was no accident, so I prayed, 'Lord if you want me to have one of those delicious coffee cakes, let there be a parking spot open right in front.' Sure enough, the eighth time around the block, there it was!"

That one hits close to home for me. We know that's no way to handle temptation. So, what do we do? We follow Jesus' example and look to him for strength. The best way to start is to walk so closely to Jesus that the call of the world has little appeal. When we are tempted, pray, utilize scripture, and busy ourselves with the things of God. Jesus is there for us in those difficult times. "No testing has overtaken you that is not common to everyone. God is faithful, and he will not let you be tested beyond your strength, but with the testing, he will also provide the way out so that you may be able to endure it" (1 Corinthians 10:13).

Jesus understands and becomes one of us to save us. That's the mystery of the incarnation.

Amen.

---

30 "Today in the Word," Moody Bible Institute, January 1992, p.32

Fifth Sunday after the Epiphany
1 Corinthians 9:16-23

For The Sake Of The Gospel

> *If I proclaim the gospel, this gives me no ground for boasting, for an obligation is laid on me, and woe to me if I do not proclaim the gospel! For if I do this of my own will, I have a wage, but if not of my own will, I am entrusted with a commission. What then is my wage? Just this: that in my proclamation I may make the gospel free of charge, so as not to make full use of my rights in the gospel.*
>
> *For though I am free with respect to all, I have made myself a slave to all, so that I might gain all the more. To the Jews I became as a Jew, in order to gain Jews. To those under the law, I became as one under the law (though I myself am not under the law) so that I might gain those under the law. To those outside the law I became as one outside the law (though I am not outside God's law but am within Christ's law) so that I might gain those outside the law. To the weak I became weak, so that I might gain the weak. I have become all things to all people, that I might by all means save some. I do it all for the sake of the gospel so that I might become a partner in it.*

Wilma Rudolph suffered from polio as a child, and it left her with a crooked left leg. She wore metal braces and had to have treatments for over six years. Through sheer diligence and determination, at the age of eleven, she forced herself to walk without braces. Her older sister was a good runner, so Wilma started to think about running which changed her life. She gave all she had to develop as a runner. She asked the coach for more practice time.

In two years, she outran every other girl in her high school in Clarksville, Tennessee. A year and a half later, she outran every high school girl in the state of Tennessee. Two years later, in 1956, she won a bronze medal in the Olympics in Melbourne, Australia. Four years later, in 1960, in Rome, she won even more taking home the gold in the 100-meter dash. the 200-meter dash, and the United States relay team. Rudolph would not be deterred. She gave her all to be able to run.

Giving your all makes all the difference. It did for Wilma Rudolph, and it did for the Apostle Paul. He was compelled to preach the gospel regardless of the circumstances. "If I proclaim the gospel, this gives me no ground for boasting, for an obligation is laid on me, and woe to me if I do not proclaim the gospel!" (v. 16).

A Calling

As citizens of God's kingdom who await the arrival of our Lord Jesus Christ, we all have a calling. For Paul, that calling was to preach the gospel. He wrote, "woe to me if I do not proclaim the gospel" (v. 16). The word "woe" indicates an expression of grief or reprimand. It was a part of who Paul was that he proclaimed the good news of Jesus Christ. All Christians have a mission or a way to serve the kingdom. Until Jesus comes back, we are to be using our gifts that way.

Elijah Lovejoy was an editor, schoolteacher, and Presbyterian clergyman. During the early 1830s he left the pulpit and returned to the press to be sure his words reached more people. He was dedicated to the cause of the abolition of slavery. Lovejoy attacked slavery and the racial system that allowed human rights abuses to go unpunished. His writing stirred up many in St. Louis. His coverage of the May 5, 1836, lynching of a black sailor charged with killing a white deputy brought out his enemies. Lovejoy condemned the killers and the judge who showed leniency to them. He fled to Alton, Illinois, but the mobs from St. Louis followed him. They attacked him ruthlessly and destroyed his presses. His friends pushed him to compromise. He replied, "If by compromise it is meant that I should cease from my duty, I cannot make it. I fear God more than I fear man. Crush me if you will, but I shall die at my post." He was killed by pro-slavery mobs on November 7, 1837.[31]

Be true to your calling and stand firm. Elijah Lovejoy did. Paul did, too. Will we?

Do What It Takes

Paul acknowledged that he was free, but was willing to become a slave to all, if necessary, to win them to Christ. He was willing to be a Jew to win the Jews. He would become under the law to win those under the law. For those outside the law, he became like them to win them to Christ. To the weak, he became as weak. He summarized it well. "I

---

31 Paul Simon, "Elijah Lovejoy," *Presbyterian Life*, 18:13, November 1, 1965.

have become all things to all people, that I might by all means save some" (v. 22).

Paul did whatever it took to reach people for Jesus. That's passion. We hear the phrase, "methods change, but the message never does." That was embodied by Paul's life. He would start with people, wherever they were, and attempt to lead them to Jesus. Whether it be the Athenians (Acts 17) or Agrippa (Acts 26), Paul was willing to identify with his listeners to gain a hearing with them.

A story is attributed to Dwight L. Moody that addressed the motivation for doing what it takes. One Sunday a woman was inviting children to come to Sunday school. She talked to a boy and asked him why he walked so far, past so many Sunday schools, to get to his own. "There are plenty of others," said she, "just as good."

He answered, "They may be so good, but they are not so good for me."

"Why not?" she asked.

"Because they love a fellow over there."

Love prompts us to reach out to people and do whatever it takes to proclaim the gospel to them. As we wait for Jesus' second coming, we need to do a spiritual inventory. We should ask ourselves some questions.

— What is it that I'm passionate about that others need to know?

— What is it that I am so compelled to do or say that I'd be willing to die for it?

— Do I love enough to act even when it isn't comfortable?

Do what it takes.

Amen.

Transfiguration Sunday
2 Corinthians 4:3-6

The Glory Of Christ

And even if our gospel is veiled, it is veiled to those who are perishing. In their case the god of this world has blinded the minds of the unbelievers, to keep them from seeing clearly the light of the gospel of the glory of Christ, who is the image of God. For we do not proclaim ourselves; we proclaim Jesus Christ as Lord and ourselves as your slaves for Jesus's sake. For it is the God who said, "Light will shine out of darkness," who has shone in our hearts to give the light of the knowledge of the glory of God in the face of Christ.

In the movie *The Polar Express*, when Hero Boy, Hero Girl, Know-It-All, and Billy escape from the sorting room, they watch as the elves hang the bells on the reindeer, Hero Girl comments on their beautiful sound, much to Hero Boy's confusion, who still cannot hear them. She and Billy then get excited at Santa's arrival, but Hero Boy's view is blocked by the stacking elves. "I can't see him. I can't see him," Hero Boy exclaimed.

There is something important about seeing the one you have come to see. For Hero Boy in *The Polar Express*, seeing Santa and getting the first gift was huge. Seeing the long-awaited King of kings is far greater. Those who are perishing cannot and will not see the light of the gospel of the glory of Jesus. However, to those who know Jesus and are awaiting his return and his kingdom, they will see the glory of God in the face of Christ. What does it mean for us to see the glory of Christ? Let's take a look.

We Have Purpose
Paul noted that he and his companions were "your slaves for Jesus' sake." The word for "slave" here literally was one who served another. Paul and his companions were slaves of Christ on behalf of the Christians in Corinth. Paul wrote that we are to present our members as "slaves of righteousness" (Romans 6:19). The task of a follower

of Jesus is clear. We are slaves of the King of kings and Lord of lords. That is our purpose while we await his return.

John Kenneth Galbraith, in his autobiography, *A Life in Our Times*, illustrated the devotion of Emily Gloria Wilson, his family's housekeeper: "It had been a wearying day, and I asked Emily to hold all telephone calls while I had a nap. Shortly thereafter the phone rang. Lyndon Johnson was calling from the White House. 'Get me Ken Galbraith. This is Lyndon Johnson.' 'He is sleeping, Mr. President. He said not to disturb him.' 'Well, wake him up. I want to talk to him.' 'No, Mr. President. I work for him, not you.' When I called the president back, he could scarcely control his pleasure. 'Tell that woman I want her here in the White House.'"[32]

Galbraith praised the dedication and loyalty of Emily Wilson. She was truly a faithful servant. Will we serve the Lord as faithfully?

We Can Know The Lord

Paul wrote, "the God who said, 'Light will shine out of darkness,' who has shone in our hearts to give the light of the knowledge of the glory of God" (v. 6). It is God who shines in the hearts of people so they can know Jesus. The creator of the universe who said, "Let there be light," shines the light of his glory in the hearts of Paul's team. God unmistakably worked in the hearts of Paul and his companions by fundamentally changing them. He empowered them to share the message of salvation. What he did for them, he still does today. We have the opportunity to know the Savior who changes everything.

Marvel Comics and movie fans know who Tony Stark is. What sometimes gets overlooked is the transformation that takes place in Stark over the course of the movie series. When Stark is introduced in *Iron Man*, he is a man obsessed with himself, who uses others to get what he wants. He has everything money can buy but has no love for anyone but himself. However, in *Avengers: Endgame*, the final movie of that part of the series, Tony Stark is different. The events and relationships he's experienced have transformed him. Stark makes a huge personal sacrifice that preserves not just the lives of those he loves but also the lives of people he's never met.

That is a fictional story, of course. Tony Stark isn't real. That kind of transformation is real, however. If you are not sure, you could ask a few people.

---

32   *Readers' Digest*, December 1981.

Ask a zealous persecutor of the Christian faith, Saul. You'll have to ask for Paul, though, since he has a new name and a new purpose.

Ask a former prostitute of Jericho named Rahab. You'll find her in the family tree of King David and Jesus Christ,

Ask a former slave trader John Newton. You will find him talking about "amazing grace that saved a wretch like me."

Transformation is one of the Lord's specialties. Paul wrote, "Do not be conformed to this age but be transformed by the renewing of the mind, so that you may discern what is the will of God — what is good and acceptable and perfect" (Romans 12:2).

Experience The Glory Of The Lord
Knowing Jesus allows us to know the glory of God in the face of Jesus. This book and series of messages conclude with a glimpse of the glory of Jesus. We began by looking at the invitation we have to be a part of his kingdom. The result of that invitation is the incredible chance we have to see the glory of the Lord.

There will come a day when his kingdom comes that the glory of the Lord will be on display for all to see. John described that day in Revelation 7. He wrote, "After this, I looked, and there before me was a great multitude that no one could count, from every nation, tribe, people, and language, standing before the throne and before the lamb. They were wearing white robes and were holding palm branches in their hands. And they cried out in a loud voice:

"Salvation belongs to our God, who sits on the throne, and to the lamb." What a day of rejoicing that will be. To be in that crowd is the kingdom realized. That is the future for all who wait for his kingdom today. So, as we conclude, we join our hearts and voices with the many who were before us and say, "even so, come quickly Lord Jesus" (Revelation 22:20).

Amen.